THE

CHATURANGA;

OR,

GAME OF CHESS.

A PERSIAN MANUSCRIPT.

DEDICATED, BY PERMISSION, TO THE

RIGHT HON. LADY ADMIRAL CAMPBELL.

BY "MRS. COLONEL HARTLEY,"

Authoress of " Indian Life, or a Tale of the Carnatic," &c. &c.

LONDON:

SHERWOOD, GILBERT, AND PIPER,

PATERNOSTER ROW ;

J. EVANS, 20, King's Road, Chelsea.

1841.

In the name of the most merciful God!

After bestowing every kind of eulogy and praise on the Creator of heaven and earth, we proceed to set forth the nature and true extent of these pages, which is this :—

One of the wonderful Tales of ABUL OLA AHMED (the mercy of the Almighty rest upon him!), in the Chaturanga, or the four members of an army, viz. Elephants, Horses, Chariots, and Foot Soldiers. ABDALMALEK, son of MARVIN NOAH BAN NASSER (may God amend his condition!), for the sake of distinctness and illustration in the Persian Language, and in order to render it intelligible to all descriptions of men, has written it in familiar and easy language, so as to combine the prosaic and poetic styles, and ordinary customs of Oriental nations : this is one of the abovementioned tales.

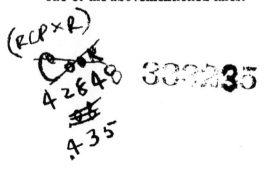

THE MARRIAGE GIFT

OF THE

HINDOSTAN SULTAN,

Supposed to be written by Abdits of Babylon, a Fabulous Legend Writer, a descendant of the same name who wrote " Historia Certaminis Apostoloci."

The peerless daughter of Sultan Ap Harsan loved the son of Benasker, the Grand Vizier; they had secretly met and exchanged vows—and they hoped fate would prove propitious, as it was customary to bestow a Persian Princess upon a favourite's son. The tongue of discord spoke loudly between the Persian and Hindostan dynasties; and to ensure a treaty from hostility, the beautiful maid of Persia was to be united to the King of the Mogul Empire—she was to have seven days to meditate upon the wedding gifts, and then for ever to leave her father's zenana for another's.

A 3

Apparently the Sophi imagined that the dark Eastern Monarch had spread a gold and silver carpet under the foot of his child, whose costly presents had decked her with jewels that as yet had never passed the royal sieve : but it was with pain that he beheld her face looking as mournful as a solitary star in a dark sky, beautiful yet desolate; her voice, so sweet and low, which sounded like the morning hymn of butterflies and bees, or the warbling of .the humming bird that lives in the cinnamon groves, was mute or trembled like the mimosa: she had received a blow more fatal than the Bahrs.* The Yakoono, although it shaded her bower with the soft looking rose apple, had ceased to shelter her from their remorseless fury. The coral shells and yellow berries still tipped the branches, and the pungent musky odours kept away the flies and evil genii from approaching her; but this tree of the Sylph's dwelling place had lost its good power in defending her from enchantment.

* Evil genii.

" Am I, who govern the universe, to have my daughter a child of sorrow? Speak, oh Benasker! and tell me why smiles not the treasure of my heart?"

" Wonder not, oh Sultan," rejoined the Vizier, " the pearl of all price looks not as placid as the silver moon she constantly resembles. She hath perused the book of her good genius, who speaks the truth; if the Hindostan Lord of the Crescent's offer be not completed, she fears her great accomplished father's life will be endangered; and to part from his care is death : therefore at his Court of Courts she wishes to descend into the valley of the shadow of death, as the phœnix, to live in memory an unrivalled queen of spices and perfumes."

" The Persian word is law," rejoined the Sophi; " look, she must read again, and quickly turn another page; this moon must shine once more through fleecy clouds of her new wedding veil: this sudden change resembles youth and beauty—nay life itself, unexpectedly extinguished in white and misty death."

" Alas! your lowest of slaves would infer,
that the matchless ornament of kings imagines
that the splendid bridegroom resembles those
shells of Ophir which wound the being whose
hands they fill with pearls.

" Her heart hath possessed that prophetic
power with wisdom gifted, for it looks into
futurity, and shudders at the picture imaged
on the glass of destiny (*Be Cheshm*). Upon my
eyes be it."

" She must see very shortly there, that if I
prize her, I prefer lasting dominion more;
although next to Persia I love my daughter.

" May her shadow be nevertheless: tell
Rhedi, the Chief of the Zenana Guards, that
I will it so—or she leaves to-morrow. Give
her this amulet¹ (Barshem Astem)."

" On my head be it," Benasker answered,
and prostrated himself before his Royal
Master as he left the Divan.

This was the first day of gloom, when
the vampire of Despair spread his heavy
leathern wing over the murky clouds that
shadowed the fair Elcaya; and the great
owls of affliction shrieked their dull fore-

bodings in her ear, in that everlasting twilight of the mind which dreads a coming evil.

Fond thoughts like parasitical plants clung round her heart until they nearly choaked the parent that had produced them. Grief had pitched his tent at the door of Affliction, and had found entrance, as the tale unfolds.

THE MARRIAGE OFFERING.

The Princess of Persia is soon to be gone,
From the land of her father, the Shar of
      Ispaghan : *
Six days have passed over, the same time will
      bring
Munificent presents—a portion and ring.
Her parent hath willed it—his orders are laws;
Neither Persians, Medes, Agars, or Turkish
      bashaws
Dare oppose his stern projects, or change a
      decree,
For the bride of King Abdal his daughter's to be.
The trumpets have echoed, the silver shawms
      play,
All is placid and brilliant as brightening day.
Fair Elcaya's computed a ransom for kings,
Radiant Peri of Beauty, she wanted but wings

* Pronounced Isfawn.

To proclaim her escap'd, from abodes of the
    blest,
To astonish the earth with so lovely a guest.
Trays of silver and gold are prepared for the
    bride,
Precious jewels, in baskets of filigree wide,
With slippers all diamonds, a province's cost;
Silk, turbans, and perfumes, and what's valued
    most,
Those huge pearls from Ormus, the Assyrian
    coast:
Such large bunches, and strings of so perfect
    a size,
Shewed those sylphides that wept them had
    no mortal eyes :[2]
Her dresses were countless—her cashmeres
    were rare—
Not one thing forgotten that Elcaya could
    wear.

One snowy hand her bosom prest,
 For well did young Elcaya know
When Mythra* journey'd to the west,
And sunk behind the mountain's crest;
And Omrah comes, the Sophi's guest,
 Just as soft ev'ning zephyrs blow.

The blue and gilded lattice shook
 Its gauzy web-like goss'mer folds;†
She leant upon the golden hook,
So hard to take a last fond look;
For ill the Median maid could brook
 The waning noon-tide growing old.

How brightly rob'd, that young princess,
 Her little hands and feet were bare,
Save in their native Persian dress,‡
By Hennah⁵ stain'd with roses fresh,
And many a fairy's golden mesh
 Fretted broad bangles light as air.

A neck and bosom like the swan,
 Were circled by the angel's tear;⁶

* Persian name for the Sun.

† The lattices at Grand Cairo and Persia are made of strained gauze, painted and gilt.

‡ Nothing can exceed the diminutive links of filigree which adorn the arms and ancles of Persian nations.

Pois'd, a gold plate suspended shone,
Engravings of the Alcoran ;
On her right cheek, it rested on,
   Coquettish, just below her ear.

This little houri beam'd with gems,[7]
   The Queen of Egypt had not pow'r
To rival this fair girl of them ;
   She seem'd in some ungarded hour—
   Peri, or Sylph, or Eden flow'r
   Escap'd from realms whose vernal bow'r
For ever twines her faint emblem.

Her yellow hair, in flutt'ring waves
   Of molten gold, flow'd wildly down,
Such tresses, when a mermaid laves
   In waters o'er her sea green gown ;
Curl'd as the mountain billow raves,
And echoes through her coral caves,
Wafting her strange melifl'ous staves
   Along the ocean's verdant throne.

Elcaya ! why that rising sigh,
   And robes with purple* shading clad?

---

* Purple is the Indian colour for mourning.

A bride to put on such a die
  Will surely make her nurse go mad :
Why, child of gentleness, oh why
Should a plain question make you cry,
  And look the saddest of the sad ?

Oh ! nurse, of love and pity hear
  The strangest story ever told :
A tale of wonder—terror—fear,
  The cruel truth will soon unfold :
Yes, sorrow wakes the silent tear,
  For Osmond's life perhaps is sold :
Sit down by me, 'tis almost dusk,
I'll whisper thoughts of love and musk.³

Shouldst thou invent a perfect box,
As smooth, and strong, like ocean's rocks—
Whether of pearl, or ivory tusk—
Within it place insid'ous musk ;
I ween that subtile captive frees
In spite of bars or bolted keys.
Then bosom thoughts as lightly prest,
Enshrin'd within the lover's breast,
How deep soe'er his secret cell
The laughing archer breaks the spell ;

So musk and love, however seal'd,
Sooner or later are reveal'd.
Giants have never chain'd the wind
Or strove the sportive boy to bind;
He will break loose all-pow'rful love,
Deride their pains, and mount above
The od'rous scent, and youth restrain,
They breathe their souls and snap the reign.

I am the musk, and Osmond love,
    We both are pow'rless you can tell;
How can I speak? he dare not move,
    Or burst this tiresome silken shell.

Yet, as the story tells, I'll try
    To break this fatal bridal ring;
And with my faithful lover fly
    Swifter than cuts the eagle's wing.

But I must woo thee, gentle nurse,
    Before arrives that Indian steed
That brings with it my fatal curse,
    Hindostan's king to wed a Mede,

To seek around the Sophi's Court,
    And find my love when all alone,

To whisper, not to leave the fort
   When first the herald trumpet's blown.

But if he quit this busy scene,
   Elcaya is for ever lost;
He must keep up his usual mien,
   Or her propitious star is crost.

And now I'll tell thee how I knew
   Osmond, the very soul of truth ;
When first we met I felt, too true,
   Existence hung upon the youth.

Nurse, fancy's like the cocoa tree,*
   Although its stem be fixt to earth,
Still a deep passion for the sea
   Will lean to where it first claimed birth.

Shining in one eternal flame,
   Our hearts, two threads of vivid light,
The older, Zella, we became,
   Entwin'd themselves in one as bright.

Mythra had spread his crimson cloak
   Over the sky, to hide those rays

* Cocoas are invariably found near the Indian sea coast ; it is a Persian simile of affection, as dear as the cocoa and sea to each other.

That from his splendid fi'ry yoke
   Had made our azure heav'n one blaze.

Fast was he sinking to his rest
   Within the river's cooling verge ;
When by the scorching heat opprest,
   I long'd to see the moon emerge.

But first of all, upon the mat,
   Sat soft Sultana purring there ;
You know my matchless Persian cat,
   With shining eyes and silken hair.

I heard a low and rust'ling sound,
   Turn'd and perceiv'd with great surprise
She'd started off—made but one bound—
   And at the open bird cage flies.

You gave my little fav'rite pet,
   The tutti Namah* green and blue ;
Upon the tatti† he was set,
   When pooni‡ pounc'd, away he flew.

I call'd her back, 'twas all in vain,
   A freak she never took before ;

* Parrot.   † Indian blind.   ‡ Cat.

And minded not, though in a strain
　　That coax'd her often o'er and o'er.

The more I held an almond high,
　　Loftier flew his painted wings;
At last he sought the open sky
　　And louder grew his chatterings.

Nurse of my soul, if you had seen
　　The cat and bird—it was a sight—
Her eyes they flam'd an em'rald green
　　When tutti Namah bent his flight.

Go, fly, outrun each willing page,
　　I beat the treach'rous spotless foe;
They took the now deserted cage,
　　'Twas vain they let poor green-coat go.

There on a lofty tow'r it perch'd,
　　Then bounded over yon deep stream,
All night our myrtle grove was search'd
　　Until the sultry morning's gleam.

Forgetful of the evening dew
　　In every maze I wandered on,
Thick flow'ring shrubs I posted thro'
　　Hoping to find my much lov'd one.

Their glitt'ring tops I ceaseless shook,
   Roses and woodbines all entwined;
I sought each beauteous bow'r to look,
   Tutti Namah I could not find.

Within the garden grows two elms,
   Their sides adorn'd by vineyard fruit;
There did I rest—grief overwhelms—
   Tir'd and fatigu'd by my pursuit.

What did I see shoot by the wall
   Of murmuring Irac, clear and deep?
Ten splendid youths so straight and tall,
   Their oars did timely measures keep.

Robes all of gold and zaphir trim'd
   Gleam'd as the swift barge gently mov'd,
And as the polish'd surface skim'd
   Reveal'd the form of him I lov'd.

He cast one upward look and past—
   It was our faithful Vizier's son—
The rowers hurried much too fast:
   Thus our acquaintance first begun.

Again unwitness'd there we met,
   When earthly sons at midnight rest;

Soon as the ev'ning star was set,
  Osmond became my anxious guest.

Hours were minutes! nay, moments days!
  Like yonder moon too bright to keep:
For once I trod the Peri's maze,
  And never thought I e'er could weep.

But sunny hours, like night's cold dew,
  Will ever wet the dryest plains;
So sorrow pierc'd my heart in two,
  These weeping eyes dissolv'd in rain.

My royal father orders me
  Another lord, Hindostan born;
I dared not own—no longer free—
  I hold his proffer'd hand in scorn.

Nurse, love has eyes and also ears,
  To one like me, so long confined;
Who quickly sees, and equal hears
  Each whisper on the babbling wind.

You must to love prove now a tongue,
  To speak and save me from despair;
Seek him on whom my fancy's hung,
  And tell him all my deep-deep care.

There is a grand impassion'd flow'r,
  That fondly gazes on the face
Of our immortal solar pow'r,
  Until the hour that stops his race.

There is no love but what will speak
  At the first glance of shining eyes;
How poor their language, oh ! how weak,
  If they reveal not where he lies.

This heart and soul he gently gain'd,
  I am the plant and he the sun ;
My every thought is fondly chain'd,
  Our sand of life together's run.

I know how well he can profess
  To bend the bow or guide the spear ;
Tell him the Persian plays at chess
  Far better than most strangers here.

Bid him engage this hateful king,
  Let me be stak'd upon Fate's die ;
Under my windows cushions fling,
  There I will view th' hostility.

This lattice looks upon the scene;
  My flutt'ring thoughts and lips shall guide ;

Through the twin'd arbour's shelt'ring green
　Will murmurs whisper by his side.

Hearken, oh nurse of my soul,
Takdeer, Destiny, after all is what we must
　　　look to;
Hem—dum ! we are one breath,—listen.

In gay apparel's splendid dress
The simple seek for Happiness;
Through temple gay and gilded shrine
I sought her form divine.
'Twas vain to seek what could not last:
Scar'd by false shadows flung around,
She only smil'd upon the past
And never will be found.

Long, long I sought her, you may guess,
And Hope, who 'tends young Happiness.
But when I question'd, half afraid,
Uncertain spoke the blue ey'd maid.

The sylph had fled all human pray'rs,
To a far purer fane
Recall'd; and shunning mortal cares,
Will ne'er return again.

Others I saw, the good and wise,
Intent upon self-sacrifice;
Yet strange no other off'ring laid,
A turtle dove, or gift display'd.
'Twas vain in fleeting scenes like this,
To find her build a home;
No! she prefers the bow'rs of Bliss,
In worlds that are to come.

One altar rose, whereon 1 leant,
A simple pot of incense burnt;
The light festoon or garland gay
Upon the table lay.
This flow'ry wreath appear'd to me
Oblation made for infancy;
Here then, I think, I cannot miss
That fairy form call'd Bliss.

Again deceiv'd—an only child,
    Some mother's tender hope was gone;

c

The angel Azrael had beguil'd
  Her lovely little son.
He bloom'd and blossom'd but a day,
Then sought again his kindred clay ;
Thus born upon her magic ground
That's never to be found.

Once more I saw a maiden fling,
Upon the shrine, her wedding ring ;
Here then, she said, I cannot miss
Gay laughing Happiness ;
She was deceived—young Love no more
Would linger on that magic floor :
He follow'd, fled her empty isles,
Chill'd in its empty whiles.

No temple then, or lofty fane,
Shall ever bring her back again ;
A hundred circles have gone round,
Yet not one spell is found.
The painted pictures she portrays
Are false as her perfidious gaze ;
The more her stay we fondly press,
Less lingers Happiness.

THE THIRD DAY.

THE INDIAN BRIDEGROOM'S ARRIVAL.

The Shar Arpen Apharson was determined to confound and astonish the Hindostan Mogul, Abdalla Ben Mahomet; and strict orders were ushered, those of the Medes and Persians which alter not, that the temples, priests, viziers, omrahs, troops, people and chariots, horses and cattle, should make their finest appearance, and wear their last holiday suits upon the day of his expected coming; accordingly the world moved in countless thousands night and day in the streets and plains, the week anterior to the Indian King's arrival: one moment you beheld along the Chaham Bagh* flying camels, mules, and dromedaries, moving in every direction,

* Chaham Bagh, the high street of Ispaghan.

with different tents and temporary erections
for the collected troops, some loaded with
preparations for a golden sea of fireworks,
which was to turn night into morning, and
spread another canopy of stars over the
upturned heads of the admiring multitude :
here you saw the poor peasant bending under
the weight of fresh-gathered fruits, beetle and
tobacco leaves, grass and sweetmeats for the
Bazaar, or the asses and beasts of burden
accompanied by the country people tottering
with innumerable cages of poultry, peacocks,
pigeons,   Mazandein   pheasants,   storks,
jungle and water fowl, mountain partridges
and game of all sorts ; others driving flocks of
sheep and goats for food ; pastry cooks were
baking and   mincing their condiments of
spice, saffron, and turmerick from their various
houses, which, open-fronted to the street,
scented the air and drew crowds of children
and flies around their dwellings ; each trade   .
was similarly occupied, and no subject discussed but the magnificent marriage of
Achmet and the Persian Princess Elcaya,
moon of moons, and the flower that never

fades. Upon the herald's sounding his approach, it was impossible to describe the imperial dress of the Sultan, or his Lords in their purple robes and embroidered garments, escorted by or heading the innumerable troops all wearing myrtle garlands upon their heads —their javelins and scimitars flashing sheets of lightning as they strode onwards, as well as the forest of spears, all bearing at the extremity a golden pomegranate; and nine thousand which enclosed them in the same manner, pomegranates of silver. A thousand of the first and noblest Persians attended the august King of men, who rode out to meet at the gate of the city of cities, the Shar's future son-in-law, all bearing spears according to the custom of their country; and a thousand horse selected like the former immediately succeeded; then came the beforementioned ten thousand soldiers of the sun's attribute, and their guards of silver, equally adorned with a seed of his ray's creation; those who proceeded trailed their weapons; then this legion was followed by an equal number of Persian cavalry, at an interval of

about two furlongs, followed by a numerous
host of regular and promiscuous multitude : in
the midst, drawn by eight matchless milk-
white horses, rolled the chariot of the sun,
mounted high upon wheels of silver, the body
of wrought ivory and gold, blazing with
jewels ; a sculptured sun, his face and rays
beautifully figured, guarded by the magnificent
Satraps ; they had made propitiatory offerings
to the parent of light, whose temple consisted
of as many pillars according to the number
of the days of the year ; it was a noble
theatre, and ornamented with double rows
of cedars, and enchanting walks circularly
planted ; the stories of the building were repeated one above another, and on the top of
the cupola open to the sky, for the sun to be
seen through ; these matchless columns were
white and gold elegantly fluted.

The edges of the flutes with the capitals
varnished all gilt ; the inner roof of the vast
galleries on these pillars were painted with
the sun, moon, and stars, expressing their different motions, with hieroglyphics known only
to the priests. The outsides of all were also

twice gilt, as was the dome, or grand concave, on the top open in the middle to the
sky. In the centre of this concave was a
golden sun, hanging in the void, and supported
by golden lines, or rods, from the edges of the
dome. The artificial sun looked down as if
it were shining upon a globe of earth erected
on a pedestal. Magnificent stair-cases, with
gilt balustrades, were also seen sweeping down
from the galleries above them.

On the pedestals of the columns were en-
graven the same mystical figures.

Then the procession of the chief priests
came chaunting hymns to the praise of Mythra,
clad in gorgeous dresses, spangled with mimic
suns; this flame-coloured attire belonged ex-
clusively to the chief.

The first order sported those of a bright
green, the second a fiery red, the third yellow, and the fourth purple.

All these represented the seasons : spring,
summer, autumn, and dark winter. They
marched in grave and dignified order, with
consecrated urns of the purest gold in their
hands, redolent of every odour.

The clang of trumpets, drums and cymbals, accompanied with the Crescent bells, shook the earth when the Mogul and his retinue, equally sumptuous but foreign to the Persians, drew up and halted at the city gates. Then roses were scattered, and wreaths of flowers were strewed in the way; and pieces of gold thrown to the people, who fought for them as they passed from the golden basins and trays that contained the Tomums, borne by Numedian slaves dressed fantastically in leopard skins, with rich bracelets, nose and ear-rings, which shone brilliantly upon their brown skins. It was a day marked by a white stone, and every beard was new dyed—and every beggar had a breakfast of currie and rice; and the sun never set that day, for so glorious a sunshine was imitated seldom ever seen before, from the lamps, flambeaus, fires, and illuminations which were burnt, and still continued to blaze at the city of Ispaghan.

Mortals had flown to bless the sun[9]
Before his daily race begun ;
The eye of day unclos'd to blaze,
And add fresh incense to his rays—
C'lestial, perfect, newly born,
Shot lambent fires around Ispaghn,
As o'er the mountain's crest he burst,
Parent of light created first :
Irac, Agemi, wat'ry floods unfold
His sacred image stamp't in gold ;
All nature shines—men's voices raise
One hallelujah in his praise.
The hills rejoice, the country blooms,
Off'ring her grateful rich perfumes :
The rosy dew in countless pearls
Silvers those wings young morn unfurls,
Who bids each Mede, with rev'rence low,
Bend with the crowning myrtle's bough,[10]
And strew large branches on the way
To hail the glorious god of day :
Soon as he topt the highest ridge
Of misty rock, his sacred bridge,
The Sophi sought the river's side
To pour libations on the tide.

A golden vessel's purest urn
Contains ten thousand sweets that burn;
There holy woods, and leaves of trees,
Each herb that blossoms for the bees,
Emblem of him who toils for man
And daily journeys heaven's bright span,
All perfect mixt, all fragrant blown,
Its odours on the waters thrown,
Essence meets essence earthly flown,
First wash'd before its final flight
Rais'd by the pow'rful fount of light.
Dew is the image of the soul,
Which mounts and seeks th' ariel goal;
A goblet[11] this imperial king
Is seen by watchful crowds to fling,
With Persian weapon, to the deep;
After the cup shall brightly leap,
The off'ring's giv'n—that duty done,
Then priests will chaunt the rising sun.

Father of all Eternity!
    In thee we see
The fountain of infinity.

Shine, great and mysterious birth,
    The prostrate earth
Now mourns her inferior worth.

Pure eye of light, whose fiery age
Is written on Time's pristine page,
In burning letters from the hand
Of Him who bid thy rays expand,
To gladden all beneath thy beams
Who dwell on earth, on sea, or streams.

Sole shadow of all perfect light,
    How bright thy sight!
Emblem of majesty and might.

Praise be offered, praise be giv'n
To the glorious God of heaven;
Praises to him, who paints the bow,
Or bids the opaled prism glow;
Directs the flashing lightning's play,
Creates the moon a softer day.

Her temper'd light reflecting thine,
    Long may it shine,
Best perfect work of night, divine.

As round thy paths of liquid blue
    Thy footsteps flew,
Bath'd in celestial dew.

Still pour upon this rolling ball
Soft incense, as each step shall fall,
Pour it on the meads and flowers,
Or those fructifying showers
Which shall promote the growing grain,
And the rich loaded bough maintain.

Shine, dread fountain, unrevealed,
On this pure oblation sealed.

Our sacred urns behold,
Cast in thy circle's mould
Of pure unchanging gold.

Incense breathing, flow'rets sighing,
Roses on the æther dying.

Storax, frankincense and myrrh,
Cedars sweet, and stately fir,
Amber, each who breathe a soul
Centre in this sacred bowl.

Scarce had the holy chorus ceast,
When a faint cloud obscur'd the east;
Curl'd just beneath the meeting sky
Where heav'n and earth seem'd one grey die,

Upon uncertain ground,
The mist appear'd to upward shoot,
Like the mild vapour from sharoot
 In eddy circles wound.
Sometimes it moves, at others heaves,
A thousand forms on fancy leaves,
Still lengthen'd miles the sight deceives,
 No true decision's found.

Each moment stronger thicker gains,
Ascending smoke obscures the plains
As sand storms shake the deserts drear,
Shew coming cavalry are near,
 When hoofs that hot soil fling
In clouds of dust upon the breeze,
Shrouding from view, men, arms, and trees,
 Just as those volumes cling,
So fast and swift these objects shone,
And sudden too, like tempest flown
To scatter tulips newly blown,
 And lay them with its wing.

A thousand gaudy heads thus seen,
White, red, and yellow, blue and green,
 Float faint, a gay parterre;

D

In lost disorder forward fly,
Now gleam to view, as quickly die,
   Just pencil'd on the air.
Like rushing waters in their course,
Sounded the tramp of many horse;
Strange foreign sounds, outlandish cries,
Distinctly on the winds arise,
And hosts are seen like countless flies,
   In armour* rich and rare.

They come! they come! all voices ring;
It is, it is, the Hindostan king,
   With all his glitt'ring band.
Hark! there is distant music, drums,
Approaching legions, distant hums,
   Pace slowly onward, grand!
For lines too bright to look upon,
Seem ev'ry moment come and gone,
A silver stream advances on,
   As if from fairy land.

Eternal chaunts, like some great bird
Of songs, in cadence now are heard
   To mingle with the rest.

     * The Ancient Indian Chain Armour.

The Nizim's army clear is seen,
In his rich varnished palanquin,
   The long expected guest.
Venetian blinds, with sliding door,
Four men behind, the same before,
Carry two poles, and deafening roar,
   Who change when hardly prest.

There yellow floating banners spread
A silken curtain o'er his head,
   In Oriental pride,
Reclines with all the pomp of state
That on Mahratta princes wait,
   When they thro' journeys glide.
Then cowries wave, and beauteous dies,
Made from the peacock's starry eyes,
Form'd into fans of giant size,
   Spread round him far and wide.

Shawls, turbans, sash of golden threads,
And silver-headed creeses,[12] sheds
   Their lustre to the sun;
With shell-work head-gear, curiously,[13]
Arab steeds rush furiously,
   Breast plated in the same.

Black housings, broider'd o'er and o'er,
Their silken reins and saddle store,
    Shine one entire flame !
Some are half pearls, some solid gold,
Others their scarlet manes unfold ;
All with a platted tail uproll'd,
    Move fetter'd to look lame.[13]

They bear the Mollahs, fierce and proud,
How stern they eye the Persian crowd,
    Grave as the prophet's mien ;
With beard and wrinkled forehead high,
Whose sparkling orbs vindictively
    Launch their sharp arrows keen.
Some peer through shawls of holy dye,
Green is the hue ; all running by
Have slaves, who hold most dext'rously
    A spade-shap'd taper screen.

And many a proud grave Mussulman,
Seid, Shieck, Mogul, besides Patan,
Ibrahem Mirza's Tartar race,
With Habeeb Mohoud next in grace,

After the Vizier past;
Princes, Ameers, of Kurrapah,
Young scions of a great Sirdah,
   All four of Turkish cast;
Fat men, whose shoulders broad display
Large muslin vests, silk trousers gay;
Self-satisfied, they seem to say,
   Here we've arriv'd at last.

Numbers on numbers onward flow
To Der Khoneh,[14] in pompous show,
   And enter first Ispaghn;
See how they take that street which leads
To Irac's fav'rite gate; their steeds[15]
   Have sweetmeats to them thrown.

Heralds announce the Sultan soon,
Great brother of the sun and moon
Arrives before the hour of noon,
   The bearers sped at dawn.

The running footmen, two and two,
Are following fast, a motley crew,
   Deck'd all in tissue dress,
D 3

And tall and heavy on the way
Are steeds from Cutch, those iron grey,
　　Now rearing from the press
Of multitudes, a startling throng,
Playing strange pipes, or noisy gong,
Careless of danger, glide along,
　　Two million, more or less.

Then Pah endaz is spread each room,
With gold brocade and rich perfume,
Red broad cloth reaches far and near,
Till shawls unite it in the rear:
　　From whence you catch a view,
The royal musnud's beauteous pall,
One rich Angora's costly shawl,
　　Of patterns fresh and new,
Imploring at the city gate,
Crowded by patient heads who wait
To see the bridegroom come in state,
　　Where he must follow through.

As the procession nears the goal
Shew yellow flags, and every soul
In wonder shouts, and all outvie
Who shall salam, or loudest cry ;

Our face is white, once more
The kus is beat, bells minstrelsy,
From crescent settings are tost high,
    And braying trumpets pour;
The man of men's enamelled whip,
Stuck in the girdle round his hip,
With step erect, and pursing lip,
    Precedes the king before.

How many miles have toil'd from far
The wond'ring tribes of Malabar,
There many men and maidens walk
In simple dress, and loudly talk,
    Some follow in a mass,
A drapery of Dungaree
Is o'er the person sported free,
    By every Indian lass;
Her shining hair caught in a knot,
Round which bright yellow flow'rets dot,
If distance takes them from their cot
    Sometimes an urn of brass.

Married, perhaps a fav'rite child
Upon her hip is carried wild,
    No tie protects it there;

It is another useful arm
That all the poor in countries warm
    Lend to the toiling fair :
Then follow numbers, old and young,
    Their throats with beaded necklace strung,
Loud bangles to their footsteps rung,
    All have some guardian care.

Perhaps a sack of Patmore rice,
Small doodies begg'd, or country pice,*
Their mats and coco' ware beside,
Or useful chatty broad and wide,
    With bag of charcoal store ;
Oft heavy doolahs creek behind,
With loose white canopy o'erlin'd,
    Low, curious carv'd before,
Drawn by fair bulls whose graceful horn
Are tipt with brass, and bells adorn ;
These jingling chime from night till morn,
    Rolling turn o'er and o'er.

'Twere vain to tell of them who made
A figure in this vast parade,
    And several Satraps frown,

* Halfpence.

Age whisper'd enemies or friends,
This, famine on the country sends
   By all these coming down,
Sad wasting devastation draws.
A pestilence with coming shahs,
Can we find rice for all these maws,
   Whole nations black and brown?

The shots still fire, the guns salute,
The Prince goes by, no creature's mute,
Tents are constructed, not one span
Of ground is left without a man
   So thick and dense they press;
Elephants, cattle, not a tree
But mourns the weight humanity
   Hath made its branches less;
Wine for the host in torrents flows,
The tired Sophi homeward goes,
Bridegroom and suite all seek repose,
   All hasten to refresh.

THE BANQUET.[16]

Amidst parterres and beds of flowers that brought the delighted and astonished king of Hindostan towards the front of an elegant building, belonging to the asylum of the world, which faced the deep lake opposite the zenana that contained the matchless princess, spread an enamelled lawn; art and sculpture were displayed with a lavish hand, for this beautiful carpet of nature led to the entrance of the palace; and its fine stately walls were supported by light polished shafts, airy devices, highly finished entablatures, and other singular and fanciful decorations; everything calculated to give pleasure and repose, magnificence or ease, was truly concentrated.

Upon entering between groups,[17] formed in ivory, representing processions in honor of Mythra, wood nymphs, and beauties of the

floods, he found himself gazing upon matchless pictures representing Bacchante subjects,
and the wild effects of the enchanting grape ;
the gentle fairies' mixed dance, and the lover's
sweet retirement, and expressed in such lively
colours that they seemed to the eyes of great-
ness as moving life.

From this gorgeous apartment a door
opened into a spacious rotunda, lighted from
the top by the sun, supported by twelve pillars, emblematical of his circular journey
round the earth.   The Commander of the
Faithful beheld a bath, round it were as many
doors which led to an equal number of sofas ;
there slaves in fanciful dresses hastened to
attend him.   The prepared waters were redolent of perfumes, warm and sweet scented.
His princely wardrobe had been duly displayed, and ten eunuchs stood ready to re-
clothe in the most sumptuous garments the
King[18] of men ; who selected an imperial emerald green suit, adorned with bunches of
roses and myrtle twigs of silver, and flowers
of pearl ; besides robes tied with extraordinary sized ones, and fastened by diamond

loups; also bordered with the rarest sable from the confines of Siberia or Thibet.

From hence he entered into a spacious saloon; where, under a canopy of gold, reclined the Sophi of Persia. Every jewel glittered, and a thousand plumes waved and gracefully danced to the breeze as they gently fanned the most magnificent of Sultans. His court shone one star of perfection. Sofas of the richest velvet, silken canopies, carpets of matchless hues and shades, cornices, mosaic walls of the most singular description, inlaid with gold and precious stones and rare woods, all struck the various senses with amazement.

Sweetly sounded Lydian measures from the galleries, supported by numberless pillars of rare red and yellow, or green marble, beautifully grained and intermixed. A hundred unseen choristers in masquerade habits were singing the pleasures of music, love, and wine; roses and violets were scattered around; the tables were spread in an adjoining saloon, still longer than the former: there shone a golden dish for every object,

E

and an equally costly cup for every guest, mixed with the wonderful porcelain vases brought from Maurigama, of such excellent staining and transparent hue, that the opal and satin could scarcely be clearer; silver was the least valuable article displayed, amongst innumerable santal baskets and filigree work, wherein stood fruits more like rubies and topazes, than articles for food. Cooling liquors, cakes, creams, and wines were spread upon gathered orange flowers; and large tubs of these odorous plants were occasionally disturbed, and emitted a rare and intoxicating perfume : soft music stole through the whole apartments, whilst at the upper end of this enchanting saloon, seated in the Palace of Delight, sported in the graceful dance the Almahs who accompanied the Hindoo Monarch's train. These queens of amusement lent too the aid of their voices, sweeter than the kokila* when she reposes upon her eggs.

Inside the Royal Ark, belonging to the

---

* The Indian Nightingale.

King of Men, was seen the Royal Stranger, the Commander of the Faithful, who wore the matchless ornament of emeralds[19] sacred to the bridegroom; and it shone conspicuous in the front of his rolled turban of India muslin. Upon his entrance, a deafening concert of cymbals, bells, and other warlike instruments increased the pomp, and welcomed his approach. The Sophi rose and embraced his son-in-law, and complimented him with a tongue of honey—then placed him upon a throne a little lower than his own.

Then a herald proclaimed that two musicians were desirous to shew their skill in poetry and song; and the powerful of the most powerful demanded the chosen subjects. An obsequious slave, prostrating his head three times, repeated, that the most humble of inferiority were ready to descant upon love, music, and wine.[20]

"The first," replied the Shar Arpen Ap Harsen, is a poor theme, which lasts as many nights as days—music, unless it be stunning, never good for anything.

" Let the coming subject be in praise of
wine.   Melek Al Shoherah* approach !"

Accordingly two minstrels stepped forward,
one a Persian, the second a Mahomedan ;
they held in their hands a venah, which is
the Indian lyre, and touching a few chords,
the former commenced as follows :—

Arise !

Why then delay ?

Time far too swiftly flies,

Let ev'ry tinkling cymbal play,

Loud clashing answers to the poet's strains,

Melting his quivering heart, firing his nervous
veins.

Shall I inhale its spirit, happily languish, die
My fleetly winging soul in heavenly ecstasy?
Must she return to shadowy earth, far, far
from rest ?

Come, soothing wine, and revel in my breast;

To a delighted world thy vintage bring;

Its praises let me gay

Discoursing sing.

Arise !

* The Prince of Poets.

Speed !

Now then behold

Me with light measures lead

His mazy footsteps tipt with gold,

And rosy purple honours of the vine.

Let us the same around our youthful brows
entwine,

Or quickly press their fragrant juices in the
inspiring bowl;

Pure essence quaffing, wakening each
slumbering soul.

Lively companions, busy let us haste,

Life's bab'ling fountain freed,

The nectar taste :

Speed !

Cream,

Stream !

Dream

Of delight and sweet delusions,

That Wit inspires

And Fancy fires;

Ever breathing soft effusions.

Will wine our mortal woes requite ?

Yes, wine will put them all to flight.

>   Roll,
                  Bowl!
                  Soul
         Of the vineyard's purple bowers,
              Then quickly pass
              The inspiring glass;
     That pearl of time's light fleeting hours,
     Wine the red—the rich and glowing—
         Wine uncork to overflowing.

                  Wine,
                  Shine!
                  Mine
         May it be to sing in rapture,
              Her golden eyes
              And witcheries.
     As we sparkling glances capture,
         Mythra stamps by his decrees
         Vine the princely king of trees.

" By the Prophet! a good song, and well sung; let it be marked upon satin, with golden ink," cried the Sultan! " and his name recorded. How does the slave call himself?"

Fordousi, the Persian Poet.

" Then let Fordousi receive a miscal of gold for every verse, and stuff his mouth with sugar candy : his face is whitened to-day—may his fame be nevertheless, or any other singer surpass him : let him style himself the Malek Al Shoheroh, or Prince of Poets : comes there any more of them ? "

The Mahomedan came forward and bowed his head three times, and remained afterwards motionless, with his hands crossed upon his bosom.

" Speak," says the Sultan !

" The lowest of your slaves wishes to sing before the Centre of the Universe, a song in praise of the pomegranate and rose, which the followers of Mahomet consider as the pearl of fruits as well as flowers; what would Sherbet be without its fragrant dew ? the Sophi also delights in its cool refreshing draughts, and disputes sometimes with the vine which should yield the preference."

" Sing," rejoined the Sultan of Persia ; " let us see and hear all about it, and judge for ourselves."

After prostrating himself three times before

the royal throne of gold,"¹ the poet exclaimed,
" Oh be the glory upon my own head ;" and
Fordousi began chaunting as follows :—

Oh, Roses of Schiras have ever been sang
  By the Persian and Arab, all poets agree
That their bloom to the eye, with the nightin-
      gale's tongue,
Forms songs for the lover, and sweets to the bee.

Attar Gul! Attar Gul! Mythra's* spirits
    impart
  Those sparks of his presence which mount
    to the brain ;
That essence of Paradise floats round the heart,
  As the cup of Elysium distils its sweet rain.

Sons of mirth and felicity, roses are blowing,
  The time is to gather—let the dew pass
    around :
Yes, the hue of ripe peaches, bright nectar is
    flowing ;
  Collect these red leaves as they fall to the
    ground.

---

* The Rosa Solis, in Persian, is the Sun's dew, a favourite
sherbet beverage.

The queen of the garden, Sultana of Flowers,
  The bird and the Persian's ecstatic delight,
To quaff thy sweet odours, or build in thy
      bowers—
  To die on thy bosom, or wreathe thee at
    night !

The bees, how they love thee ! thy lip is dis-
    tilling
Fresh honey for them, in thy cup they are lost.
If birds of the ether delight in thus filling,
  No wonder earth shares in their pleasures
    the most.

If I rifle thy charms, I am mad in so doing,
  To scatter in pieces a fragrance so lost ;
Here trickles the diamond, the ruby is brewing,
  Thou pearl of all price is dissolv'd to my cost.

Yet, again thou wilt blush as thy fair flow'r
    changes,
  When pouring forth sherbet through cool
    crystal shrine,
'Tis better to catch thee whilst death ne'er
    estranges
  Thy all-powerful soul in a generous wine.

Farewell to the grape so often forbidden,*

Our Prophet was right when he bid us refuse,
Attar Gul! Attar Gul! that secret tho' hidden,
Is reveal'd, for in thee we have nothing to lose.

"That rogue is a very pleasant fellow,"
exclaimed Shar Arpen Ap Harson, "but he
is quite wrong when he declares the Prophet
denies wine (La Ellah Ellallah Mahomed
reful Ollah), there is no God but one God,
and Mahomed is his Prophet. He did not
do so—for see our beautiful Niskhi manu-
script of the Koran, in red and black ink,
most splendidly illuminated, belonging to the
royal library, says nothing about it; yet, it is
entitled the marrow of interpretation—the
cream of commentaries—the flower of ex-
positions. Other nations must have had the
sleep of the soul when they perused the
Koran. The blessed City of Yezd, and the
true worshipers of fire, believe Ali sent wine
to comfort them for the loss of our Prophet,
Bis Millah." The King of Kingdoms stopped

---

* The Persians and Mahomedans are forbidden in the Alcoran
ever to touch wine.

short, for he saw a potentious frown collecting upon his future son-in-law's brow, and prudently forbore to press the forbidden dispute further, lest it might lead to a political quarrel. He therefore was contented with expressing himself equally well pleased with the Turkish Poet; and in compliment to the king of Hindostan, ordered him a silver robe, and ten pieces of gold.

The increasing heat of the day dismissed the assembly, and it was time, for the Brother of the Sun and Moon looked eclipsed with angry darkness; and the Sophi's eye of light, a huge diamond, which entirely composed the crown of his turban, appeared to nod in an undignified manner to the beg le begs, and stars of his court, no doubt shaken off its balance by the unsteady foot of majesty, who in vindicating the right of drinking wine had too fully discussed the point by suiting action to the word; however, he was kept in countenance by the august multitude around him, whose staggering steps and half-falling movements afforded risible amusement to the Turkish guests, who felt that

their quiet and sober demeanour most re-
sembled the dignity of Allah, and that the
Persians were but men much lower than the
angels; and that were they in their mosques,
there would not be wanting Turks with whips
and sticks to keep the Omrahs in order.

"I do not think," whispered the Indian
king, Abdalla Ben Mahomet, to his vizier,
"that the Shaikhulislam is the best lawyer, or
the Persian Mujtahids have improved them.
I would not give a whiff of my hookah for
any of them; they are Khur'be teshdeed
(doubly accented asses)."

"The Commander of the Faithful possesses
the penetrating eye of the lynx."

"And the wisdom of the elephant," replied Selim, the well-beloved vizier.

"It is true (Beshem Ustem); upon my
head be it. What can I say more?"

* The Shaikhuislam is the principal administrator of law;
there is one of these officers in every city, and a Cadi in subordi-
nation to him. The chief priests, or Mujtahids, have a great
undefined power over the courts of law: the judges continua'ly
submit cases to them. In all Moslem courts of importance, the
Cadi is assisted by several Moollahs, or learned men.

THE FIFTH DAY.

A PERSIAN HUNT.

The Princess of Persia sat in the Pavilion of Delight, in the Pàlm Groves, where the orange plants are arranged by thousands in China vases under golden latticed-work trellices, and the yellow grapes from the Casbin vineyards twine with the rose and pomegranate, and all laugh and rejoice in the sun.

The dark myrtle shaded the windows, and formed a natural jalousè; whilst the jessamine starred the earth, and wafted her mellifluous breath, mingling herself with ten thousand odours; the aloe and fig-rose, tall and stately, and the green palm, towered above all.

Sweet was the garden's bloom of Irac;

F

but not by comparison half so lovely, young
and charming, as Elcaya, the Sophi's daughter. Here she sat, with her aged nurse
Shauru, who was consoling her for her coming
departure ;[22] for neither the trays of silver and
gold, embroidered slippers sparkling with
diamonds, necklaces of pearls, rich bracelets
which had cost the loss of a province to
procure, the richest shawls from the looms of
Cashmere, nor the most magnificent muslin
and silk dresses, could extort a smile. Her
eyes bathed in sorrow, Persia's most beautiful
daughter reclined on the bosom of her nurse,
transfixed with woe.

She was the silver moon,[23] glittering in dew ;
all was as bright as the beams of Mythra, for
in three days she was to depart for the City
of Delhi, and the last day of hunting had
arrived anterior to departure this day. The
hunter's festival commenced; through her
lattice she was permitted to behold the coming
procession and festivities, and the collected
train.

Twice the silver shawms had sounded the
morning hour of dawn, and the kneeling

sumpter camels, all docility and obedience, were patiently receiving their heavy loads of numerous tents, and cheer for the venturous sportsmen; whilst the tremendous elephants, equipped with their silver hoodahs, stood throwing up the cool green benana boughs high in air, and catching them on their trunks, revelling on their long red cones, that so plentifully hung from those gigantic stems.

The chetahs[24] in couples, trained like the European greyhounds, stood decked with their jewel collars on, flashing brightly to the sun, their numerous spots darkening as they stood in eager anticipation of their prey, the bounding antelope they were to chase. The oriental topaz was not more radiant than their eyes, and the low growl, mixed with the baying of the dogs, was distinctly heard through the neighbouring courts.

Two hundred splendid Arabian steeds were seen caracoling up and down the distant plains, and the long buffalo whips, made of the rhinocerus's hide, cracked loud and fiercely over the heads of the accompanying mules and dromedaries. The Hindoo Visitors'

sicies were cooking their rice from a multitude of earthen chatties, whilst the Persians'
repast, coffee and dishes of milk, sweetmeats
and fruit, stood plentifully before them.
Their pipes filled the atmosphere with the
pungent tobacco, which both nations appeared emulous to rival each other in
smoking, and the opium dish was passed
merrily round ; as also were those sweet cakes,
sprinkled with the seeds of poppies.   Other
dishes made their welcome entrance also, and
all were beginning without ceremony to de-
vour the food with expedition.   The Hindoo
king's superb horse stood under cover of the
portico, with his rich black velvet saddlecloth
studded with pearls and diamonds, white
reins, and panache of red and yellow feathers,
with mane and tail died with the deep red
hennah juice.

By his side stood four sicies, with the huge
cow-tails, whiter than the fleecy cloud from
Bootan ; whilst the proud creature stood
champing his silver movable bit, and shaking
the same chains that adorned the rich tassels
that graced his neck; during which an old

Persian groom sung gaily, as he stroked down
an umbrageous beard long as the Angora
goat, the following canticle, an old hunting
song well known in Bokaria, from whence he
was a native :—

Who shall conquer again 'gainst me to-day?
Not the lion, he is too weak a prey :
A trusty jav'lin sends him straight away.

I never car'd with paltry deer to cope,
The blithe gazelle, or bounding antelope,
With savage chetahs they can have no hope.

Let me then, ever proud, be active found
To try my strength upon that dang'rous
      ground,
Where the wild ass comes leaping at a bound.

Him let me seek to conquer ; he or I
Must in our fearful struggle yield or die :
To win him, madly over rocks I'd fly.

His ariel home stands upward on the hill;
He scorns the bridle, and a master's will,
And guards the fountains of the mountain rill.

F 3

No curb can check the gor,*[25] or render mild ;
Sharp is his bite, and furious kicks how wild !
To catch him man must prove much more than
      child.

————

Come fly, my arrow—bend, my bow,
Swift o'er the chasm let me go ;
The wild wind shakes the flapping trees,
The quarry scents the passing breeze.
Over the river banks or mead
Bounds my courser, glides my steed ;
The saddle firm, no sultan's throne
Equals the hunter's joys alone ;
Then fast we go, still faster he,
Wild is our headlong revelry.
If round his brist'ling head I loose
The long entangled dreaded noose,
My agile foe is quickly thrown
Upon his knees, and hunted down :
Within that treach'rous, tangling cover
The game is caught, and hunting over.

————

Shrill sounds the trumpet from afar,
The suburbs look one vast bazaar :

         * The wild ass.

To-day the Sophi's thousands chase
The flying deer, and lion face;
Or the wild ass, the fiercest game
That ever hunter tried to tame.
Around the court huge boughs are seen,
Benana fruits, both ripe and green,
Toss'd by the elephants, in order
Rang'd around the ample border,
Cool'd by the wide and spreading fans
Of many tall and huge banyans;
Against each tree are sev'ral made
Secure beneath that ample shade.
Some mighty trunks are bending low,
Others mount high the tempting bough;
There sitting on the sandy ground,
The attending mahout's to be found,
Their smoking chatties fill'd with rice,
Or curried meat, dissolv'd with spice,
For morning meal, before he takes
His castle-bearers* to those breaks,
Whose clam'rous hoofs the centre shakes.
A splash is heard upon the bank,
One has broke loose, and sought the tank:

* Elephants.

Thirst hath propell'd that creature there,
Made fierce by flies and scorching air;
Pain'd, half mad, he plunges thither,
Laves, inhales a perfect river,
Then soon a hundred fountains throws
Of muddy rills before he goes,
Streaming the currents to the sun,
Until the merry pastime's done.
" Come back, my prince;" " stay here, my
     lord;"
The docile truant at a word
Returns, when call'd in gentle strain,
And walks demurely back again:
No goad nor whip could make him move,
Unless seduced by voice of love.
See now the chetahs come in pairs,
Start forth strong guarded from their lairs:
Strange chains and hoods are putting on,
The Persian dogs will soon begone.
How savage, yet how fierce they be,
And grand in their ferocity!
By hues of yellow-coloured fawn
Spotted, and view yon deep line drawn
On inner angles of each eye,
So dark engraved with self-same die.

Behold those stately necks maintain
A thin and bristly hog-like mane;
With convex profile forehead too,
And eyes that pierce you through and through;
So fierce and large, you scarcely can
Too highly prize them, from Decan,
The Eastern greyhounds hence they call,
These springing wonders from Napaul.
To chase the deer the Sultan wills,
This day they sweep around the hills,
For at their base on plains there's scope
To nimbly hunt the antelope;
And strong that hand and promptly gone
To save the game thus hunted down.
A vaulted kennel underground
Shew'd where was lodg'd each barking hound;
Cool and complete with bath and bed,
All chunum'd floors on which they fed,
A tiger race,* both fierce and strong.
Four towns untax'd maintain the throng,
Above the stables, white as snow,
Stretch long extended in a row.
Who can describe the spreading stalls,
Or measure true those lofty walls,

* See Herodotus.

That rise to shield the fav'rite stud,
Which scour wide plains, or breast the flood ;
Paint gran'ries huge of gram* and wheat,
Provisions stor'd for hordes to eat.
Here thousands in the shortest space
Could mounted be to join the race ;
Whole families within them dwell,
The countless children none can tell,
Belonging to the grooms who tend
Upon the horse, and round them wend ;
Under their feet they calmly lie,
And sleep in blind security,
Or play with golden pipes and straw,
Their fathers' badge before the shah ;
Shields in a huddled mass, and spears
Glitter in polish'd steel whole tiers ;
Wild trophies from the woods and fells,
Boars' tusks, huge skins, and tortoise shells ;
Bows, arrows, slings, and many sheaves
Of javelins, swords, and spreading leaves,
Of Burgustuwan[26] armour, skin
Well tann'd and lin'd through thick and thin ;
Protection for the steed who flies
To where the fierce-prest lion dies :

* Indian peas, or vetches.

For there unmov'd he's taught to stay
Transfixt, nor mark the least dismay.
His upturn'd hoofs and rising mane
Shew to the monarch of the plain
How well he knows his powerful spring,
And voice which makes the valleys ring;
He pants to see the javelin fly
To free him from this misery;
Matchless the rider who could wage
Such reckless war, or prompt engage
The mighty ruler of the brakes,
When coming foes his anger wakes;
But more the barb, who coolly stands
Obedient to the reins' commands.
The trumpet sounds, 'tis time to go;
Elephants' standards* fiercely glow,
Light zephyrs, as they rose and sunk,
Reveal'd their massy sides and trunk;
Then horses prance, and shrilly neigh,
They paw the ground, impatient stay.
The Sophi and the royal guest
First turn'd themselves against the west,

* The Persian standard is a most gaudy flag, with the elephant
blazoned upon a golden field.

Leap on their saddles, off they go;
To them the hunters lowly bow.
With open tongue the pack to-day
Runs blithely on, nor brooks delay:
A perfect sunshine gilds the earth,
And all looks harmony and mirth,
Save the fair moon, who, drown'd in tears,
Half tott'ring under frights and fears,
Steals to the marble urn, and creeps
Where trickling falling water weeps,
Till Osmond joins, and danger braves,
And on his hapless passion raves;
Wilder than storms or water pent
Until their fruitless force is spent.
So 'gainst a father's stern decree
How could their powerless hands be free?
'Twere vain to fly—'twere vain to hope
A star would deck their horoscope;
Still hope is nursed, and vows are sworn,
Till, waken'd by the coming horn,
They homeward seek the fost'ring shade,
The maid her bow'r, the youth the glade:
He chaunted from the Shar Namah,
This Persian stave, a fav'rite bar :—

To-morrow we renew the fight,
To-morrow we shall try our might :
To-morrow, with the smiles of heaven,
To us the victory be given.

THE STAKE AT CHESS.

When the sun descended into the west, and the moon appeared in the east, the King of Hindostan, and Osmond, the Vizier's son, sought the soft breezes of evening outside the door of the pavilion. The centre of this enchanting building opened upon a wide and spreading lawn, which was beset with more elevated tufts of the most delightful verdure; blushing and transparent fruits glowed forth between the cool leaves; here in beautiful wild disorder contained the graceful woodbine and the enchanting rose, mingling with the Persian lilac and the Arabian acacia, and contributed their several odours with the orange and myrtle in sweet contention with the luscious and aspiring grape, golden as the mine's rich store from Ophir; the Chinese pheasant, with his silver companions, ran to and fro with the king of birds, the majestic peacock, as agile as an elegant and stately nymph ; whilst the wild and sportive gazelle stood browsing on the rose-leaves, and admired herself in the crystal flood, which at the extremity of the scene ran gently washing the margin, and seemed to freshen every object as it passed.

. A grove of myrtles, which led into shady mazes,[27] wreathed with jessamines, passion-flowers, and syringas, covered the brown trunks of the trees, lighter than the Maraboo feather ; in the midst of which appeared other matchless buildings which decked the river side.

There, under a spreading fig-tree, fenced by as large a cedar, overshadowing the Princess Elcaya's window, reposed her lover and betrothed royal spouse, and the fatal game of chess was to decide who should obtain her hand. Osmond the skilful, blessed by the geni of Hope, had already won three hundred purses, as many huns and pieces of gold. The dark king had sworn, during that fatal hour the sherbet cup had passed the royal lip, to win the coming battle, or lose the

Princess, whom he staked upon the Chaturanga Board, for ever.

They made a most charming and majestic
appearance, and an awful solemnity charac-
terised and accompanied their gestures,
which forcibly struck the heart, and sponta-
neously demanded the reverence of every
beholder.

The Sophi will not stir to-day,
Dismiss the court, send all away;
And let no tattling voice be heard,
Death waits on them who speak a word.
Bring here my costly Chatrang*[20] board,
With all the gold and jewell'd hoard:
Set out in ranks those knights of fame,
A lordly pair to play the game.
The silent mutes submissive bring
That santal chest before the king,
Who opes the box, displays the bed
Where slumber chiefs both white and red;
The cotton down, in perfum'd rows,
Shews burnish'd knights and sleeping foes,

* The Game of Chess has been immemoriably known in Hindostan by the name of the Chaturanga, or the four members of
an army, viz. elephants, horses, chariots, and foot soldiers; by a
corruption of the pure Sanscrit word, it was changed into
Chatrang.

So costly that each radiant stone
In thousand brilliant sparkles shone.
The Attar Gul* was sprinkled round,
Each dew drop fell and cool'd the ground:
The gold and ivory board inlaid,
Was spread beneath the fig-tree shade.
Two tap'stry cushions soon were found,
Of well stuff'd leather, red and round,
Placed for the Sultan on a mound,
On close cut turf, above the guest,
Who on another gently prest,
And half reclining on his hand,
Waited the bright allotted band.
First rose the matchless ruby king,
The Vizier† takes the right hand wing,
His robe of yellow topaz shews
And rivals quite the saffron rose.
The trotting Phil,‡ in measur'd pace,
Prepares to take his forward race;
The ponderous Hodah's silver seat
Reveal'd the Mahout's safe retreat;

    * Otto of Rose.
    † The Queen was called by the French, and after them by the
English, during the middle ages, Fierce, Fierges, Fiers, derived
from the Persian word Pherz, or Phirzen, a minister, vizier,
counsellor, or general.
    ‡ Phil, or Fil, the name of this piece upon the chess board,
which signifies an elephant. The French nation changed it to
the modern Fou.

That fort upon his golden back
Was worth an oriental lac,
For resting on his well-built neck
A stately castle's seen to deck,
Mosaiced in a thousand forms
Of stones, beside bright silver shawms
Display their two-fold power for storms;
Then em'ralds studded all the towers,
And countless pearls, like minute flowers
Strew'd o'er the housings' velvet store,
As myriad stars print heaven's bright floor.
Fair ivory tusks th' elephant rears,
And ear-rings hoop his drooping ears;
Then rich in gems of scarlet hue
The gaudy camel starts to view;
Ruch* is he call'd in Persic tongue,
With sweeping step he moves along;
Like speed of light so swift he goes,
So straight and fleet to meet his foes:
His eyes are made of beryl's stars,
That flash upon these feudal wars;
The rising hump, with em'ralds gay
Shot vivid halos from Cambay;

* Ruch, sometimes spelt Rokh, the dromedary, or camel,
changed to the castle.

Mixt sapphires blue, the deepest shewn,
Like lotus lilies newly blown.
With locket hung by golden chain,
Enrich'd with treasures from the main,
Rattled in costly trappings free,
And flash'd a principality.
Another piece, gay Aspen Suar,*
Rises upon the chequer'd floor,
Ah! who could shew so fine a steed
Or aim a truer sharp gareed,
As this dread soldier at a need?
Jewel of jewels, gem of gem,
All that was fine appeared with them,
In perfect shape to meet the sight,
And prompt to stem the desp'rate fight.
Then comes that pale and beauteous king,
The ruby's foe, no ostrich wing
Was ever fairer than the tooth
Which form'd the fragile iv'ry youth;
Diamonds surround his head in streams
As moonlight quivers glitt'ring beams.
In opal dress one shower of pearls,
White Pherz a golden sash unfurls;

* They made the horseman called Aspen Suar, cavalier or knight.

Elephants are on the border,
His camels also range in order.
Tourquoise and opal, topaz, and
Those rare deep garnets from the land
Of Ceylon, or of Samarcand,
Shone as the others did before
All filigree in precious ore.
Two milk-white steeds start forth for fight,
One for the king, one Phirzen's knight;
Then soldiers seven, in or-molu,
Emboss'd by pearls and sapphire blue,
Stood proudly forth in goodly row,
To fight or fall, as chance may go;
The same again, in silver cast,
Makes up the given number last;
The warriors rang'd, 'tis time to draw,
Fortune decides, for that's the law,
Who should commence the mimic war.
The rose unto the lily yields;
First Osmond stirs the battle field,
Upon his Lord this favour fell,
A loss the Sophi fears too well;
The royal pawn takes measures too,
Then halts and proudly stands to view;

The silver foe does just the same,
It is the order of the game.
Red* royal Phil takes that fourth square,
Next to this Vizier's own compeer :
This the opponent copies too,
It is the safest thing to do.
White elephant's silver pawn now stirs
That one that guards fair Vizier Phirz,
One step, or else he sadly errs.
The sanguine monarch's fav'rite horse,
To aid th' elephant without loss,
Rides to a third square on the course.
Pale Vizier's pawn, at double pace,
The coming foe begins to face ;
Then falls to die, for ah ! his life
Yields to the ruddy soldier's strife ;
Another friend, of argent hue,
Pierces the foeman through and through.
The regal elephant in haste
Takes the third square upon the waste,
Close to the crimson Vizier's knight,
Who holds command within his sight ;

* The red king's pawns were gold, the white king's silver.
Beydal is the Persian name for them.

That silver horse the vizier rides,
This prudent step his thought decides,
Three squares from argent Phil divides:
These stand, or in an evil hour
Too soon would fall the nodding tower.
Now see the flaming monarch tall
Passes behind the camel's wall;*
Secure he stands in this retreat,
Safe from the raging battle's heat.
The faithful white knight half a ring
Within two paces guards his king;
Opponent elephant's body guard
Attempts the uplifted stroke to ward;
One foot he moves, this danger shuns,
Then white Phil to his Vizier runs
Three squares, and stops a coming blow
Red Phirzen's soldier aims to do;
Cautious two given steps, an ace
Had nearly stopp'd his marshal pace;
Again the imperial soldier moves,
The red knight round the monarch roves,
Now hurls keen darts to guard the throne;
The gen'ral's fort is seen alone,
At three squares off the shadow's thrown;

* The king castles.

A guardsman of the white tower forms
Another square, then onward storms.
The silver Vizier close repairs
To watch and guard his second squares ;
Brave Tower Ward of crimson Phil
Strikes the white foe, intent to kill :
He conquers, dies that warlike man,
But soon reveng'd, a vet'ran wan
Defeats him, well the flowing tide
Of life no longer's seen to glide.
The gen'ral's Phil, of sanguine hue,
Constantly keeps his king in view,
Three times four angles measures too.
Four doth the white knight do the same,
For foemen war, and broadswords flame.
The impetuous scarlet Vizier flies
Close to his king, two footsteps rise,
Open he takes them, truly wise.
Now battle rages, evil hour !
Down falls to white the crimson tower ;
Yet see, a private takes the fort,
As stubborn as the mountain ghaut ;
The red king seeks his trusty wall
Behind the camel strong and tall ;

Horsemen and camels, soldiers fight,
They swiftly move as rays of light;
Or when dread lightnings rend the sky,
And heaven assumes its darkest die;
When the fell bolt strikes but to wound,
Or root the teak tree to the ground.
Th' elephant's uprear'd trunk annoys,
The trampling steeds of knights destroys;
See the wild charger, like the wind,
Sweeps bounding over thrown mankind;
His arching neck and furious eye,
Tell how he loves the battle cry.
The dromedary's footing sure
Still keeps his given ground secure;
Patient he waits each dread command,
As if he trod his much lov'd land,
The fiery desert's scorching sand.
Then how the mahouts'* sound alarms,
From their shrill clarions, silver shawms;†
Throughout the field they spread alarms.
The gold and silver pawns now close,
Thick is the fall of deadly blows;
Both red and white are seen to hurl,
Their various evil weapons whirl;

* Elephant drivers.　　　† Indian trumpets.

II

With pell-mell fury on they go,
O'erwhelming castle, vizier, foe,
'Tis difficult to say who gains,
Or loses on those battle plains.
The golden pawns their last blood shed;
Excepting two the silvers fled:
The crimson king has still the best,
Two camels and his vizier rest;
Whilst the fair royal youth in prise
Hath nearly lost himself, and sees
Destruction hover o'er his fate,
The coming of a twice check-mate;
— For there, fettered in the trammels
Of twofold misery's crushing camels,
And the red vizier at a word
Will strike and wield his lifted sword;
No intervening power can stay,
His vig'rous arm, or e'en delay
That falling ill; an only tower
Still shelters at this fatal hour;
And one' poor ruch is kneeling down,
Half dead with toil and nearly gone;
Two distant soldiers prisoners are,
They cannot aid him in the war;

When lo ! a silv'ry voice above
Attentive cried, " I've watch'd thee, love ;
Oh ! cede thy camel in this strife,
And thus from death preserve thy wife."
'Twas done, and Osmond won the Ring,
Exclaiming, " Sha hem,* O my king !"

* Check-mate is derived from the Persian word Shat Mat (or, the King is dead). When playing with their sovereign, the Orientals say only, Sha hem (or, O my King). A certain King of Persia is said to have ordered that when a check-mate was given, they should instead of that expression say, Nefs mat, or The person is dead.

___

SITUATION OF THE GAME.

WHITE.	RED.
King 40, Rook 49, Bishop 37;	King 2, Queen 15, Rooks 7
Pawns 18 and 19;	and 50;
1 Rook, 49 to IX.	1 King, 2 1 *.
2 Pawn, 19 to 11 O.	

The Authoress has been informed, that the numbers upon the Persian and French Chess Boards do not always correspond; she therefore subjoins that of Philidor, to mark the position of the game:—

RED.

Red King at his Queen's Knight's square.
Queen at her King's Knight's 2nd square.
Queen's Castle at its King's Knight's square.
King's Pawn at his 6th square.
King's Bishop's Pawn at his 5th square.

WHITE.

King at his Castle's 3rd square.
King's Bishop at 3rd square.
Queen's Castle at its own 3rd square.
Queen's Bishop's Pawn at its 6th square.
Queen's Knight's Pawn at its 6th square.

————

ERRATA.

Page 56, line 4, for *sang*, read *sung*.
— 82, line 1, for *silver* read *ruby*.
———— line 3, for *red* read *white*.

NOTES

PERSIAN MANUSCRIPT.

~~~~~~~~~~~~~~~~~~~~~~~~~~~~~

1. *"Bind the amulet on his arm."*—It seems, by the text, that the mohreh, or amulet of Rustem, was celebrated throughout the world for its wonderful virtues, besides the Shah Namah : Solomon's seal was a talisman of an extraordinary power, said to be capable of rendering objects invisible, and of creating every kind of magical illusion ; but mohreh is more properly an amulet or spell against witchcraft.

The Shar's great diamond, which he wears in one of his amulets, is called the koh nur, or the mountain of light.

Mumiai and pahzer are antidotes in which the Persians have great faith ; the Turks and Persians believe that amulets protect them from the gins and dives (evil spirits, and the evil eye).

Tahmuras, and other ancient kings of Persia, whose adventures in fairy land, amongst the peris and dives, may be found in " Richardson's Curious Dissertation."

———

2. It is the belief of the Persians, that pearls are tears wept by the angels, which sometimes fall into the sea.

———

3. " *The Princess Elcaya, or the Flower that never fades.*"—A tree famous for its perfume, and common on the hills of Yemen.

———

4. The tents and pavilions of Eastern Princes were exceedingly magnificent; they were often made of silks, velvets, and ornamented with pearls and gold: the tent of Nadir Shah was made of scarlet broad cloth, and lined with satin, richly figured with precious stones.

———

5. This practice is common all over Bengal, Hindostan, Persia, Turkey, and as far west as the Mediterranean; all the ladies die their nails a rose colour, supposed to

be used to compliment youth, by representing that of the dawn ; and also allegorically for a ray of the sun. Vide in the note to the first line of the second book of the Odyssey, edited by Clerk.

---

6. The ladies' dress differs in Persia little from the men's, but is much more expensive, owing to the ornaments which they make use of: among these, are a gold or silver plate suspended on the right cheek, just below the ear; on this plate is engraved a prayer in the Arabic language.

---

7. Both the ladies of Turkey and Persia outvie each other in the astonishing cost of their clothes and jewels; the former were described as wearing long spangled robes, open in front, with drawers, or pantaloons embroidered in gold and silver, and covered with a profusion of pearls and precious stones, which display their persons to great advantage.

Their hair hangs loose, and flowing in very thick tresses on each side of their cheeks, falling quite down to their waist, and covering their shoulders behind ; these tresses were quite powdered with diamonds, not

displayed according to any studied arrangement, but
as if carefully scattered by handfuls among their flowing locks : the two nations resemble each other mate-
rially in costume. The Authoress beheld a beautiful
Persian Princess, with a (Tooti Namah) small talking
parrot upon one finger, and a large Persian cat at her
feet.

---

8. The Persians declare, that neither the passion of
love, nor the scent of musk, can ever be disguised, but
will invariably betray themselves.

---

9. " Of the theology of Zoroaster, which was darkly
comprehended by foreigners, and even by the far greater
number of his disciples; but the most careless observers
were struck with the philosophic simplicity of the
Persian worship."—GIBBON.

Summits of the highest mountains appear, intimated
by Scripture, to be chosen places for divine worship.
And it is not to be wondered at, that the oracular
temples were for the most part situated in mountainous
districts, is a remark made by the celebrated Vanhale;
and who also supposes that such elevated spots were

best chosen as the most proper theatres for the display of religious enthusiasm.—See Deuteronomy, chap. xii. ver. 2, 3.

The worship of the ancient Persians had unquestionably been very early corrupted; the reverence paid to the sun, and to fire, which Zoroaster appears to have considered merely as representatives of Omnipotence.

" The fountain of light seems to have been an idea too refined for the gross capacities of the vulgar, who with regard to the great invisible prototype, turned all their thoughts to the adoration of those ostensible deities." —RICHARDSON.

" The Guebres are known by a dark yellow colour, which the men affect in their clothes."—THEVENOT.

" The Ghebers generally built their temples over subterraneous fires. Among the Ghebers or Guebres, there are some who boast their descent from Rustam. —STEPHENS, Persia.

" Tahmuras and other ancient kings of Persia, whose adventures in fairy land, amongst the peris and dives, may be found in Richardson's curious dissertation, respecting the ceremonies of the Ghebers, round their fire, as described by Lord. The Daroo, he says, giveth them water to drink, and a pomegranate leaf to chew in the mouth, to cleanse them from all inward uncleanness. Early in the morning the Parsees or Ghebers, at Oulam, go in crowds to pay their adoration to the sun, to whom, upon all the altars, there are spheres consecrated, made by maji, resembling the circles of the sun;

and when the sun rises, these orbs seem to be inflamed,
and to turn round with a great noise; they have every
one a censer in their hands, and offer incense to the
sun."—RABBI BENJAMIN.

The curious reader will find all the different kinds of
ancient chariots and other carriages, enumerated and
explained, in "*Montfaucon's Antiquities.*"

THE CAR OF XERXES.

" The Monarch will'd, and suddenly he heard
His trampling horses, high on silver wheels:
The iv'ry car, with azure sapphires shone,
Cærulean beryls, and the jasper green,
The emerald, the ruby's glowing blush,
The flaming topaz with its golden beam,
The pearl, the empurpled amethyst, and all
The various gems which India's mines afford
To deck the pomp of kings—in burnished gold
A sculptur'd eagle from behind display'd
His stately neck, and o'er the royal head
Outstretch'd his dazzling wings; eight generous steeds,
Which on the fam'd Nisan plain were nurs'd,
In wintry Media drew the radiant car.
——————————— At the signal bound
Th' attentive steeds, the chariot flies behind;
Ten thousand horse in thunder sweep the field;
He now draws nigh—the innumerable host
Roll back by nations, and admit their Lord,
With all his satraps, as from crystal domes,

Built underneath an arch of pendant seas,
When the stern power whose trident rules the floods,
With each cerulean deity ascend,
Thron'd in his pearly chariot, all the deep
Divides its bosom to the emerging God—
So Xerxes rode between the Asian world—
On either side receding."—LEONIDAS.

Ancient Scimitar.—"It was natural enough that the Scythians should adore with peculiar devotion the God of War; but as they were incapable of forming an abstract idea of a divine or corporeal representation, they worshipped their tutelar deity, under the symbol of an iron scimitar."—GIBBON.

---

10. "*Branches of Myrtle.*"—The myrtle was with the ancients a very favourite plant, and always expressive of triumph and joy; the hero wore it as a mark of victory; the bridegroom on his bridal day; and friends presented each other with myrtle garlands in the conviviality of the banquet.

Harmodius and Aristogiton, before-mentioned, when they slew the Athenian tyrant, had their swords concealed beneath the wreaths of myrtle; of which incident,

as recorded in a fragment of Alcæus, Sir William Jones
has made a happy use in his poem to liberty.—Beloe's
Herodotus.

"*Kus*" is a timbal or large brass drum, which is
beaten in the palaces or camps of Eastern princes.

---

11. Whether Pagan libations were still continued
at a more modern data, in Persia, is unknown : certain
it is mentioned, that Xerxes poured into the sea a liba-
tion from a golden vessel, when the sun appeared ; and
then addressing it, he implored him to avert from the
Persians every calamity.

---

12. A good description, taken from the representation
of British India. The large man on the grey horse,
with the shawl turban, gold threaded sash, and silver-
headed creese (or dagger), to whom they are salaaming,
is a native of some distant province, not perhaps under
our authority ; the housings of his horse you see are
embroidered with gold, his reins silken, the animal too
has a breast plate and head ornaments of shell work ;
the servant running by his side holds that spade-shaped

screen always to shade his face, and the man himself, though looking vain as well as proud, has a free, cheerful self-satisfied air : not so the Mollah or Mahomedan priest. Mark his iron-grey beard, and wrinkled forehead, and those fiercely-sparkling eyes, alive and youthful, with a feeling of hate. What an insolent vindictive look he casts at us! he recollects (for he was a young man then) when in the year 1780, the cavalry of Hyder Ally rode shouting through the gardens of our countrymen, and recollects too, that he wished them success.

The Tucomans are of the Suni persuasion; with them green is a sacred colour, but it is not so among the Shiahs. The Khena is used for the hands, feet, and hair; the Surmeh is a collyrium.

---

13. The native Princes and Chiefs fetter the two front legs of their horses until they acquire the custom of jumping forward like rabbits, this is supposed to look imposing and consequential in their gait.

---

14. " *Der Khoneh.*"—The gate of the palace, where public business is transacted.

I

15. An istigbal, composed of fifty horsemen of our Mîhmandar's tribe, met us about three miles from our encampment ; they were succeeded as we advanced by an assemblage on foot, who threw a glass vessel filled with sweetmeats beneath the envoy's horse, a ceremony which we had witnessed at Kawzeroon, and which we again understood to be an honor shared with the King and his sons alone.

---

16. Feasts from three, four, five, or six days, often continued without interruption. This seems to have been an ancient practice previous to the commencement of any important undertaking, or at the setting out of a journey.

---

17. The Palace of Darius, at Persepolis, a celebrated city, then the capital of the Persian empire, contained all that was magnificent, or the arts (known at that time) could design or portray. It was afterwards laid in ruins by Alexander, who civilized Persia, and left to posterity a fine Grecian taste, particularly for painting ; his artists' carvings in ivory and curious sculpture are still remembered by comparatively modern historians ;

but time has swept away those fine specimens, despoiled
by barbarism, and hardly are they now recollected by
the worshippers of Ali, who, like the Turks, obey the
commandments of Mahomet; and respect to a fanatical
degree the second commandment delivered to Moses on
Mount Sinai.

18. The Persian and Turkish monarchs delight in
hyperbole :—" May he live a thousand years ;" " May
his shadow be nevertheless the centre of the universe;"
and the "King of Men," are eternally rung in their ears
when addressed by nobles and subjects.

19. The jika is an upright ornament worn in front of
the crown: Indian bridegrooms invariably wear it
during their notch or wedding ; and it is also an insig-
nia of royalty.

20. Of wine in every age the Persians have been ad-
dicted to intemperance, and the wines of Schiras have
triumphed over the law of Mahomet.

21. Kai Kaus, the second King of Persia, of the dynasty called Kainnides; he succeeded Kai Kobad, about six hundred years B. C.; his throne was of pure gold.

---

22. Amongst the nations of the East nothing can be done without presents between the parties, whether the negotiation be a political, commercial, or of a domestic nature.

We learn from a passage in Genesis, xxiv. 22, that the bracelets of the Orientals were remarkably heavy, which seems in some measure to justify the sentiment of the Ethiopean Prince, who thought them chains, simply because they were made of gold, which was used for that purpose in his country.

---

23. *" My heart becomes as slender as the new moon."* Eastern nations delight in comparing female beauty and their heart to the moon.

---

24. Field Sports in India.—The mode of coursing, with the chetah, is thus described :—

"They are led out in chains, with blinds over their eyes, and sometimes carried out in carts; and when the antelopes or other deer are seen out on a plain, should any of them be separated from the rest, the chetah's head is brought to face it; the blinds are removed, and the chain taken off. He immediately crouches and creeps upon his belly; should the chetah miss his aim, he desists from further pursuit, and slinks back to his master, who replaces the hood, and reserves him for another chance. When he is successful, the ferocity of his nature at once displays itself; so that to recover the prey, the keeper is obliged to be extremely cautious, enticing him with meat, carried for that purpose. These beautiful creatures are rare in collections in this country; but the menageries of the Zoological Society contain three or four specimens. The fur is more than moderately full, and of a yellowish fawn colour, the paw is less rounded than that of the cat, and in form is more approaching to the dog, beautifully covered with round black spots, and a distinct stripe of this colour passes from the inner angle of the eye to the mouth; a thin hog-like main runs down the back of the neck; the forehead and outline of the profile are convex : the eye is very fine, large, and expressive."—Colonel Sykes's Catalogue of Animals found in the Deccan. He observes, domestication produces a difference in the fur of the chetah, which has led to the supposition, that there are two different species. The wild skins possess a rough coat, and in which the mane is marked; while domesticated animals from the same part of the country are destitute of mane, with a smooth one almost touching the ground, until he gets within a short distance of the deer, who, although seeing him approach, appears so fascinated, that he seldom attempts to run away. The chetah then makes a few surprising springs, and seizes him by the neck: if many deer are near each other, they often escape by flight—their number, I imagine, giving them confidence, and preventing their feeling the full force of that fascination, which, to a single deer, produces a sort of panic, and appears to divest him of the power, or even inclination, to run away or make resistance. It is clear that they must always catch them by stealth, or in the manner I have described, for they are not so swift as common deer.

---

25. Onager or Gor.

" Hunting the Gor or Wild Ass appears to have been a favorite sport in Persia. Bahram the Sixth was surnamed Gor, in consequence of his being peculiarly devoted to the chase of this animal, and which at last cost him his life."—D'HERBELOT.

An Arabian author says, " The best place in the world is the saddle of a rapid courser; the best friend in the world is a good book."

Persians had a mode of carrying their quivers behind or under their shield.

When Tritantæchmes, son of Artabazus, was appointed to this principality by the king, he received every day an artaby of silver. The artaby is a Persian measure, which exceeds the attic medimnas by about three chænices; besides his horses for military service. This province maintained eight hundred horses, and sixteen thousand mares; he had, moreover, so immense a number of Indian dogs, that four great towns in the vicinity of Babylon were exempted from every other tax but that of maintaining them. — Vide Herodotus.

---

26. The armour called Burgustuwan almost covered the horse, and was usually made of leather and felt cloth.

In the hunting excursion, most of the hunters are completely armed with spear, sword, shield, mace bows and arrows.—For a history of the ferocious Indian hunting dogs, see HERODOTUS, Cliv. page 260.

---

27. The beautiful arbours referred to in the MS. are often included within the walls of Eastern palaces; they are fancifully fitted up, and supplied with reservoirs,

fountains, and flower trees. These romantic garden pavilions are called Kiosks in Turkey, and are generally situated upon an eminence near a running stream.

---

28. I suppose brought from the Holy Land, one of the thirteen jewels of Britain.

The Chess Board, Gwenddole ab Ceidio, if its men were placed upon it, they would play of themselves ; the chequers were of silver, and the men of gold.

A very old Norman Poem, upon Chess, is translated from page 149 in this manner :—

The Chess Board is thus, never was less ;
The lists are of fine gold, artfully molten ;
The pawns of emeralds, as green as a grassy field,
The other of rubies, vermilion like ardent fire ;
Kings, fers, knight, alphin, rook, and *Cornu**
Were made of sapphire, and with moulded gold,
The others of topaz, with all their virtue ;
They are beautiful to behold, arranged and expanded.

* I know not the meaning of Cornu, unless it may be Cornet, or box, wherein the pieces were kept ; on a Chess Board of gold and silver, plays with his knight.

J. Evans, Printer, 20, King's Road East, Chelsea.

Lightning Source UK Ltd.
Milton Keynes UK
UKHW020645090223
416652UK00001B/51